The Invisible Presence

The Invisible Presence

Meditations to Help You
Praise, Pray, Think, and Smile

By Eleanor Isaacson

Copyright © 2020 by Eleanor Isaacson

Unless otherwise indicated, Scripture taken from NEW KING JAMES VERSION BIBLE® (NKJV). Scripture taken from the New King James Version®. Copyright © 1982 by Thomas Nelson. Used by permission. All rights reserved.

Marked Scriptures taken from NEW INTERNATIONAL VERSION BIBLE® (NIV). Scripture taken from the Holy Bible, New International Version®, NIV®. Copyright © 1973, 1978, 1984, 2011 by Biblica, Inc.™ Used by permission of Zondervan. All rights reserved worldwide. www.zondervan.com The "NIV" and "New International Version" are trademarks registered in the United States Patent and Trademark Office by Biblica, Inc.™

Eleanor Isaacson Publications

https://www.eleanorisaacson.com

ISBN 978-0-9991374-1-3

Book and E-book designed and formatted by
www.ebooklistingservices.com

1 3 5 7 9 10 8 6 4 2
Printed in the United States of America

Dedication

It has been said...
Good friends are God's way of taking care of us.
Carol Fausel and Barbara Zagier have proven
that for many years.

Acknowledgements

I wish to acknowledge important people in my life who helped shape me into the woman I am today.

My **Aunt Lisbeth** who raised me from age 2 to 13 during the war in Germany, under the Hitler Regime and then Communism.

Fred Mackenzie was a wonderful caring and quiet Elder in the Assembly in N.J. He nurtured and guided all of us into a close walk with the Lord. His knowledge and commitment to Christ was contagious and his fatherly image made us all feel secure. Thank you Uncle Fred.

George Sharp was another gifted and very outgoing Elder in the same Assembly in N.J. He also nurtured and guided us into a consistent walk with the Lord. He had a beautiful voice and his singing inspired all of us to look forward to being in heaven. Thanks to you Uncle George.

My parents who really tried their best to give me a home.

Marian Schroppe, who introduced me to Jesus Christ and became my mentor in my early Christian Life.

Charles Cameron, who handed me Bible verses every Sunday to help me grow in my new faith. Somehow he also served as a father figure in my life, since I never really had a father.

Hilda Trimmer, who was a joyful example and a well-groomed Christian Woman

Marian Moeller, my Grammar School friend, who helped me not be fearful in the classroom when the Fire Drill went off, and convinced me that there would be no bombs falling.

Delores Bayard, who so patiently helped me learn to ski and introduced me to young Christian Groups.

Barbara Zagier, who found her Messiah through my widowhood and has given me lots of joy watching her mature in her new found faith for the past 25 years. We have bonded so well and talk weekly on the phone.

Carol Fausel, who came to my Bible study in 1989 and has grown by leaps and bounds in the knowledge of our Lord Jesus Christ since. We have a wonderful bond and Carol is a wonderful Sounding Board for me. We chat weekly on the phone.

Jeanette Windle, editor extraordinaire, who makes my books easy to understand. She is fabulous.

Amy Deardon, of ebooklistingservices.com, who is my formatting angel.

Bob, my scientific husband. Last but not least, your love and devotion has been the most nurturing element in my life. Your encouragement over the years has given me the courage to speak and write to this day. Bob, you're no longer here on earth but I know you would be pleased. Still love ya lots.

Table of Contents

Introduction

The Invisible Presence has its inception in my book *Dancing from Darkness*, which tells the story of my childhood living through the horrors of WWII Nazi Germany as well as the continued drama of coming to the United States as a young teen. Throughout my many speaking engagements, people have been inspired by and wanted to know more about my encounter with the Invisible Presence who made Himself known to a lost little girl and kept me sane even when I had no idea of just who this living Presence was. A Presence I would eventually come to know by other names—heavenly Father, loving God, Prince of Peace.

In response to those people, this book is a compilation of meditations on God, faith, and my own spiritual journey along with many of the specific scriptures that have nurtured me and helped me grow in my faith and into a deeper intimacy with the heavenly Father who is endlessly teaching me new and wonderful things about Himself. The purpose of these meditations is to make the reader praise, pray, think, as well as to smile. God does have a sense of humor, and we need to recognize that and laugh with Him. So I've included some humorous thoughts and readings as well. I trust you will enjoy, digest, and pass them on to others as well just as I am doing in this book.

So, dear reader, enjoy the journey as we begin.

Part One:

Meditations to Help You Pray and Praise

He shall be like a tree
Planted by the rivers of water,
That brings forth its fruit in its season,
Whose leaf also shall not wither;
And whatever he does shall prosper.
—Psalm 1:3

Indwelt

Jesus said: "Ye are the salt of the earth . . . the light of the world."
—Matthew 5:13-14

Notice in this verse that neither salt nor light make noise. We should be encouraged to shine for the Lord without having to speak a word. The following words titled *Indwelt* that I came across some years ago from an unknown author expresses beautifully this truth.

Not only in the words you say, not merely by your deeds expressed,
But in the most unconscious way is Christ expressed.
It's not your beatific smile, a holy light upon your brow.
Ah, no, I felt His presence when you laughed just now.
For me 'twas not the truth you taught, to you so clear, to me still dim,
But when you came to me, you brought a sense of Him.
And from your eyes He beckons me,
and from your heart His love is shed
'Till I lose sight of you, and see the Christ instead.

—Author Unknown

"Christ in you, the hope of Glory."
—Colossians 1:27

The German Bible translates this as "Christ in you makes everything glorious." So, dear believer, be yourself and trust that the Holy Spirit will shine through you.

So What Do You Think?

_____

_____

_____

_____

_____

_____

_____

_____

_____

_____

_____

_____

_____

_____

_____

_____

_____

_____

Reasonable

"Come now let us reason together, saith the Lord, though your sins be as scarlet, they shall be as white as snow; though they be red like crimson, they shall be as wool."

—Isaiah 1:18

This passage from the prophet Isaiah as he gives God's message to the people of Israel is the only place in Scripture where we read of God "reasoning." When God wants to reason with us, it is always in connection with our sins and failures. He laid all the punishment due us on our Lord Jesus Christ, who paid a heavy price when He died for us on the cross of Calvary.

Only God the Father really knows all that was involved when Jesus Christ, the Son of God, paid for our sins in full. How wonderful to know that God is always ready to forgive and cleanse when we come to him, because our Lord Jesus paid in full for our redemption. We see this promised in I John 1:9: "If we confess our sins, he is faithful and just to forgive us our sins, and to cleanse us from all unrighteousness."

So, dear believer, don't waste years of guilt and regret about how badly you've messed up. Our Lord invites you to "come boldly to the throne of grace" (Hebrews 4:16). So let's move forward in faith, accepting His forgiveness and rejoicing in His love. This doesn't mean that we have the liberty to sin because God forgives us anyway. No, this should humble us and help us clean up our act.

Jesus paid it all. All to Him I owe.
Sin had left a crimson stain.
He washed it white as snow!
—E. Hall

So What Do You Think?

_____

_____

_____

_____

_____

_____

_____

_____

_____

_____

_____

_____

_____

_____

_____

_____

_____

_____

Leaning

"Trust in the Lord with all your heart, and lean not unto your own understanding."

—Proverbs 3:5

"Who is this who comes up from the wilderness, leaning upon her beloved?"

—Song of Solomon 8:5

I love connecting one scripture with another scripture, and here is one example. We are not to lean upon our own understanding in any situation, but we are to lean upon the Lord. How very intimate this is! It is like the story of the Last Supper when the apostle John is described as leaning on the Lord's breast (John 13:23). Then in Song of Solomon we have a description of a loved bride who is coming up from the wilderness, leaning on her beloved.

When we lean on our Lord Jesus Christ, we are already on the way *up* from any wilderness we might be in. So dear believer, lean on Him with your full weight today, knowing He does all things well in your life. We are safe in His arms as the familiar hymn reminds us:

Leaning, leaning,
safe and secure from all alarms.
Leaning, leaning,
leaning on the everlasting arms.

—Elisha Hoffman

So What Do You Think?

_____

_____

_____

_____

_____

_____

_____

_____

_____

_____

_____

_____

_____

_____

_____

_____

_____

_____

_____

God Rested

"God rested on the seventh day."   —Genesis 2:1

"When he [Jesus Christ] had purged our sins, sat down."
                                              —Hebrews 1:3

What exactly does it mean that God rested? Was He sitting or reclining with nothing to do? Whatever He did, He interrupted His rest when Adam and Eve sinned. Immediately, He began walking in the garden to restore them to Himself. He walked and worked all throughout the Old Testament, ending up at Calvary.

Then when our Lord Jesus was on the cross, He said, "It is finished!" Having paid the price for our sins, He then sat down. The Trinity can now rest for all eternity. No more interruptions. Creation is finished. Redemption is finished.

So God has nothing to do today except to help you, dear believer. Give Him your problems and so give Him something to do. He is waiting to bless you!

Redeemed by the blood of the Lamb.
                                              —Fanny Crosby

So What Do You Think?

Shoulders

"For unto us a child is born, unto us a son is given, and the government shall be upon his shoulder."   —Isaiah 9:7

"And when he hath found it [the lost sheep], he lays it on his shoulders."   —Luke 15:5

How precious this image of our Lord Jesus as a Shepherd carrying His lost sheep! Isaiah's prophecy tells us that as Messiah and Savior, Jesus holds all the governments of this world on one shoulder. But when it comes to lifting up one sinner, He lays it on both shoulders. This is a reflection of just how important one soul is to our Lord. He gives more of Himself to one lost person who places their trust in Him than to all the governments, politics, programs, and

opinions of this world.

So, dear believer, take courage and trust your loving Savior to get you through whatever you are facing today. You are a much loved child. Believe it!

Safe in the arms of Jesus,
safe on his gentle breast.
—Fanny Crosby

So What Do You Think?

Baggage or Luggage

"This one thing I do, forgetting those things which are behind and reaching forth unto those things which are before."

—Philippians 3:13

Baggage or luggage? Which are you carrying around today?

Baggage is all the things of the past, good or bad, successes and failures.

Luggage is what we pack when we are moving forward. The apostle Paul, who wrote the above words in his epistle to the Philippian church, not only had to forget his old life of sin but also good things such as his education, upbringing, status in Jewish society as a Pharisee—everything!

So, dear reader, let us discard old habits, thoughts, and ideas. Instead, let's press toward the mark of the high calling of God in Christ Jesus.

Out of my bondage, sorrow, and night,
Jesus I come, Jesus I come,
Jesus I come to thee.

—Mary Walker

So What Do You Think?

_____

_____

_____

_____

_____

_____

_____

_____

_____

_____

_____

_____

_____

_____

_____

_____

_____

_____

_____

_____

The Blind Man

"He spat on the ground, and made clay of the spittle and anointed the eyes of the blind man with the clay."

—John 9:6-7

The way our Lord Jesus chose to heal varied greatly. In fact, sometimes it might seem completely unpredictable and even bizarre. In this text, he made clay with his spittle and then placed that clay on the blind man's eyes.

Why would the Lord make this man's lack of sight even darker than it already was? The blind man was already in darkness. The clay would add to that darkness, wouldn't it?

The blind man had no idea that he was about to receive a miracle.

So it is sometime in our lives. Trials become even darker just before a miracle.

Dear reader, wait expectantly and patiently for God to bring you the miracle you have been praying and waiting for.

Only believe, only believe,
all things are possible,
only believe.

—Paul Rader

So What Do You Think?

_____

_____

_____

_____

_____

_____

_____

_____

_____

_____

_____

_____

_____

_____

_____

_____

_____

_____

_____

_____

Provocation

"But the Lord had shut up her womb. Her adversary also provoked her relentlessly."

—I Samuel 1:5-6

Hannah, wife of Elkanah, was being constantly harassed by her co-wife Peninnah because Peninnah had children while Hannah was barren. Yet the Lord had a special purpose in all this provocation. It forced Hannah to make a vow and pray in earnest for a son, dedicating him to the Lord long before he was conceived and born.

When the Lord opened her womb, Hannah kept her vow. Her firstborn son Samuel became a priest of the Lord, a prophet, and in time anointed and dedicated Israel's first kings, Saul and David. Because of Hannah's obedience in surrendering her firstborn to God's service, the Lord blessed her with five more children.

Dear reader, are you being provoked by something or someone today? Be encouraged and take it all from the Lord. Maybe like Hannah God wants you make a fresh vow to Him. God is getting you ready for something wonderful.

Under his wing I am safely abiding.

—William Cushing

So What Do You Think?

_____

_____

_____

_____

_____

_____

_____

_____

_____

_____

_____

_____

_____

_____

_____

_____

_____

_____

_____

_____

_____

_____

Power of Words

"Death and life are in the power of the tongue."

—Proverbs 18:21

"With whom you find thy gods, let him not live."

—Genesis 31:32

"And Rachel died, and was buried."

—Genesis 35:19

When Jacob fled from his father-in-law Laban with his children, wives, and all his possessions, Laban accused him of having stolen Laban's household gods, or idols. Jacob swore an oath that if anyone in his household had stolen from Laban, they should not live. What Jacob didn't know was that his most beloved wife Rachel had taken the idols. Just a short time later, she died in childbirth.

So did the words of Jacob's mouth kill Rachel? This is a serious thought. Our words have power, not only when we preach the gospel, but every word we say. So, dear reader, what comes out of your mouth? Are you always complaining or constantly having an "organ recital"? Your arthritis hurts. Your stomach is acting up. Your liver is out of order. Etc.

We should instead be obeying the words of the apostle Paul in Philippians 4:8: "Finally brethren, whatever things are true, honest, just, pure, lovely of good report, if there be any virtue and praise, think on these things."

Sing them over again to me, wonderful words of life.

—Philip Bliss

So What Do You Think?

Ruth the Moabitess

"Ruth, the Moabitess..."

—Ruth 2:2

"Ruth, the Moabitess..."

—Ruth 4:10

"So Boaz took Ruth and she became his wife."

—Ruth 4:13

Ruth was the Moabite widow of an Israelite man who left her own people, country, and idol worship to accompany her mother-in-law Naomi back to Israel and become a follower of Yahweh. Throughout the Old Testament book that bears her name, she is routinely called Ruth the Moabitess, not only by Naomi, but by Naomi's closest relative Boaz and by all his workers. This changes in chapter four when Boaz takes Ruth as his wife. Her past no longer matters. In fact, she becomes the great-grandmother of King David and an ancestor of Jesus Christ.

How wonderful! We who were Gentile sinners also receive a new name and identity when we accept Jesus as our Savior. We are no longer called sinner, but Christ's bride, body, and temple, members of a chosen race and holy nation.

"But you *are* a chosen generation, a royal priesthood, a holy nation, His own special people."   —1 Peter 2:9

"Therefore, if anyone *is* in Christ, *he is* a new creation."

—1 Corinthians 5:17

More love to Thee, Oh Christ, more love to Thee.

—Elizabeth Prentis

So What Do You Think?

_____

_____

_____

_____

_____

_____

_____

_____

_____

_____

_____

_____

_____

_____

_____

_____

_____

_____

_____

_____

_____

Our Weakness

"God has chosen the weak things of the world..."
—I Corinthians 1:27

Do you ever feel like God can't use you? When I feel that way, I like to remind myself of an often quoted list from Scripture, though there are many variations and just who originally wrote it is unknown. Here is just part of that list.

Noah was a drunk. Abraham was too old. Isaac was a daydreamer. Jacob was a liar. Leah was ugly. Joseph was abused. Moses stuttered. Gideon was scared. Samson was a womanizer. Rahab was a prostitute. David was a murderer and adulterer. Elijah was suicidal, Isaiah preached naked. Jonah was rebellious. Naomi was an angry widow. Job lost everything. Peter denied Christ, Martha worried. Samaritan woman was divorced and living in sin. Timothy was too young. Zacchaeus was too short. And finally, Lazarus was dead!

And yet God used each of these people in a mighty way. Similarly, God will use our failures to create a powerful ministry in us if we are open and willing to be used. Remember, God is not interested in our successes and failures as much as in our faithfulness to Him.

So whatever God has given you to do, do it with all your heart as a service unto God. This will take the sting and boredom out of the daily grind. You won't look for compliments or thank yous from people you serve, especially members of your family. It is so wonderful and freeing. I know. I have learned this throughout my life.

Take my life and let it be consecrated, Lord, to thee.
—Frances Havergall

So What Do You Think?

_____

_____

_____

_____

_____

_____

_____

_____

_____

_____

_____

_____

_____

_____

_____

_____

_____

_____

_____

_____

The Tied-Up Donkey

"'The Lord hath need of him...' They found the colt tied by the door outside in a place where two ways met."

—Mark 11:3-4.

The colt in this passage was the fulfillment of the Old Testament prophecy that the Messiah would come riding on a donkey's colt (Zechariah 9:9). If that colt could talk, he might have been saying to himself, "Here I am watching all those people serving the Lord out on the street. And I'm stuck here tied up to a door of all things!"

Had the colt wiggled himself loose, he would have missed the greatest opportunity to serve the Lord. Instead, he became the only animal in this universe privileged to give the Lord Jesus Christ a ride into Jerusalem. Jesus needed this colt to be there tied up and waiting until the time came when the Lord called for him.

So, dear reader, are you feeling stuck? Your Lord may be getting you ready for some special service too. Just stay where you are until the Lord calls you. No more excuses. God can use you to your full potential without you even knowing it. Besides, you aren't the Message. You are only the messenger.

In the Christian life, one of the hardest things God may be asking us to do is to wait. Think of Joseph in the book of Genesis. He was in prison close to thirteen years for having done what was right. God used that wait to prepare him to become second-in-command of all Egypt. Sometimes the longer and darker the trial, the greater the ministry that awaits us. So be patient, dear friend. God is doing something wonderful in your life.

I'm waiting for Thee, Lord, Thy beauty to see, Lord
—Hannah Burlingham

So What Do You Think?

_____

_____

_____

_____

_____

_____

_____

_____

_____

_____

_____

_____

_____

_____

_____

_____

_____

_____

_____

Fatherhood

"When my father and mother forsake me, then the Lord will take me up."

—Psalm 27:10

"I am a father to the fatherless, saith the Lord."

—Psalm 68:5

If you, like me, didn't have the pleasure of being loved and cared for by an earthly father, be assured that God, your real Father, arranged your life that way. It was His way of ensuring that you will focus on Him as your Father. It will take spiritual muscles to do that. But being deprived of this nurturing relationship with an earthly father early in your life or even into the present can become an impetus for you to step out into faith for God to fill that aching loss. It works. It has worked for me in my life.

The Maker of fatherhood in all its tenderness can make it all up to you for the lack of an earthly father in your life. God has done that for me. God does make all the emptiness in our lives a beautiful stepping stone, not only in seeking an intimacy with Him, but also for a fulfilling life of service.

Look up the word "Father" in your Bible concordance and see how many verses there are related to that topic for you to enjoy and believe.

So What Do You Think?

Jealousy versus Envy

"I am a jealous God."

—Joshua 24:19

"I am jealous over you."

—II Corinthians 11:2

"Let not your heart envy sinners."

—Proverbs 23:17

"I was envious at the foolish."

—Psalm 73:3

What is the difference between jealousy and envy? Jealousy is wanting to keep what belongs to you. Envy is craving that which doesn't belong to you.

So jealousy can be a virtue. In fact, the Bible tells us repeatedly that God is jealous over us. He wants to keep us close to Himself because He has paid a heavy price to make us His own. That price was the coming of the Lord Jesus Christ into this world to redeem us on the cross of Calvary.

When we wander away from Him, God gets on our case and gets jealous. How wonderful that we are so loved that God wants to keep us to Himself. He wants us to worship Him alone. He knows that we will benefit from our devotion to Him alone.

Let's stay close to God daily, not only to enjoy His Wonderful Presence but to worship Him in all His glory.

So What Do You Think?

He Has Magnified His Word

"He [God] has magnified His Word [the Bible] above His Name."
—Psalm 138:2

Interesting! God's name is above every name, and yet this verse tells us that God magnifies His Word above His name.

The words of the Bible are sure, predictable, and trustworthy. We can use them all as a guide for our lives.

So it is in our lives also. We are what we say. Our words represent who we are. Are we living daily by what we say? We should all be people of "our word." This is called integrity!

Let's carefully use our words to bless others and not to destroy people.

So What Do You Think?

_____

_____

_____

_____

_____

_____

_____

_____

_____

_____

_____

_____

_____

_____

_____

_____

_____

God Opens Doors Automatically

"They reviewed all that God had done with them, and how he had opened the door of faith unto the Gentiles."

—Acts 14:27

Jesus Christ, the rejected Messiah of Israel, came to be the promised Savior and sacrifice for sin. And not just for Israel but for the whole world (John 3:16). God's plan has always been to include the Gentiles, as He promised to Abraham in Genesis 12:3: "In you shall all the families of the earth be blessed."

The Jewish people didn't realize there would be two comings of the Messiah. His first coming was as a humble, lowly servant dying on the cross for our sins (Isaiah 53). His second coming will be as a public, strong King whom the Jewish people will accept as their Messiah.

Here in Acts 14:27, we see that God opened the door for Gentiles to hear the wonderful message of the gospel. This message is that all people can be saved by accepting Jesus into their hearts and lives and so start a whole new life. When we believe in Jesus Christ, we are born again and become "new creatures" (2 Corinthians 5:17).

So, my dear reader, are you trying to pry open a door in your life? Stop and ask God to open the door in His good time. In the meantime, read your Bible daily and trust God, waiting on Him in patient expectation. Attend a good Bible church to build your faith. Pray to God to bring some spiritually-mature people into your life.

So What Do You Think?

A House Swept Clean

"And when he [the devil] comes he finds the house swept clean. Then goes he and takes with him seven more devils and they enter in and dwell there and the last state of that man is worse than the first."

—Luke 11:25

So it is with any addiction in our lives we are trying to overcome in our own strength. We make all kinds of resolutions and promises to ourselves. We take classes or on-line courses. We pray. We eventually reach some sort of victory and are proud of ourselves, sure that we'll never fall back into the addiction.

This works for a while, sometimes even years. We brag about our victory to friends. But then comes a weak moment, and we tell ourselves, "Oh, just once won't matter!"

This Bible verse reminds us that if we "give in" even once, we open ourselves up to being even more addicted than we were before. This is true of a recovered alcoholic. Once they taste just one sip, they are back to square one, and it will be twice as hard to stop again.

So, my friend, if you are battling with any addiction, take this to heart and don't go back. Ask God to keep you from falling.

"Now unto Him who is able to keep you from falling, and to present you faultless before the presence of His glory with exceeding joy."

—Jude 1:24

So What Do You Think?

Finished or Unfinished?

"He [Jesus] said, 'It is finished!' And bowing His head, He gave up His spirit."
—John 19:30

In the Hebrew language, there is never a past, only a present and a future. Something is either finished or unfinished. It is either perfect, imperfect, or in the process of being completed. So our salvation in Christ is a "finished work" even before we have personally received that salvation by believing in Jesus. After six hours of enduring the wrath of God against sin on our behalf when He was dying on the cross, our Lord Jesus Christ said, "It is finished!"

When we have put our faith in His finished work, we can now rest assured that we are accepted in Him. It is a gift. Our sins have been forgiven because Christ paid the price for us.

"For all have sinned and come short of the glory of God."
—Romans 3:23

"The wages of sin is death, but the gift of God is eternal life through Jesus Christ our Lord."
—Romans 6:23

Salvation is a personal gift, and we must receive it by faith. If you think you know the Lord but aren't really sure, read John 3:16 and replace "whosoever" with your own name. This verse has been in the Bible almost two thousand years. But it doesn't really do anybody any good unless they put their name in there. That is what I did back on Thursday, February 25th, 1954, at 8:45 a.m. As I did so, this verse became my spiritual birth certificate.

For God so loved the world, that he gave His only begotten Son, that **whosoever** believes in Him shall not perish, but have everlasting life.

—John 3:16

So What Do You Think?

_____

_____

_____

_____

_____

_____

_____

_____

_____

_____

_____

_____

_____

_____

_____

_____

_____

Spiritual Battles

"For we wrestle not against flesh and blood [people in our lives] but against principalities, against powers, against the rulers of the darkness of this world, against spiritual wickedness in high places [spiritual demonic influences in our lives]...wherefore, take unto you the whole armor of God, that you may be able to withstand in the evil day, and having done all to stand."

—Ephesians 6:12-13

Notice the first phrase in this verse uses the verb "wrestle." Why doesn't it say, "we box not" or some other such term? Boxers in the ring hit out and move away from each other. In contrast, a wrestler is grappling in close to his opponent. Similarly, the devil comes in close in our battles with him. His purpose is to make us doubt the love of God.

If we don't fight the spiritual battles that come up against us, be assured we will have to fight a lot more earthly battles. Maybe we decide we don't need to read God's Word daily because that is for weak people. Or we think we can handle the devil's attacks all by ourselves without spiritual armor. Not taking a stand in spiritual battles spills over into our earthly life, whether our relationships, jobs, pride in our successes, regret over our failures, lack of peace in our hearts, feeling unfulfilled in everything we do, fear of old age, fear to die.

We need to put on our spiritual armor and use the sword of the Spirit, which is God's Word, the Bible, every day. Remember, our Lord Jesus lives inside you and is with you as you take a stand against spiritual wickedness: "Christ **in** you, the hope of glory" (Colossians 1:27).

So What Do You Think?

_____
_____
_____
_____
_____
_____
_____
_____
_____
_____
_____
_____
_____
_____
_____
_____
_____
_____
_____
_____
_____

Grace

"Grace and truth came by Jesus Christ..."

—John 1:17

"For by grace are we saved through faith and that not of ourselves,
it is the gift of God, not of works, lest any many should boast."

—Ephesian 2:8-9

It may seem logical that the way to get anywhere in this world or the next is to work hard, be disciplined, frugal, positive, maintain a healthy bank account, be good, and do good to as many people as possible. But the Bible tells us that we don't get to heaven by working for it in any way. We get to heaven by simply accepting God's free gift of grace and believing in Jesus Christ who paid the price for us to go there. The problem for many people with this free gift is that they don't want to get anything for nothing. "I'm a self-made man," they may tell themselves. "I don't need a handout."

This is called human pride. Grace is not something we can earn. It is undeserved favor, and it is the only way to receive eternal salvation. If we refuse it, we lose out.

Grace is a relationship that gives us access to someone else's wealth, love, and power we can't possibly earn ourselves. In this case, God's. Believe it!

So What Do You Think?

The Devil

Maybe you think Satan has horns, wears a red suit, carries a pitch fork in his hands, and has blood dripping from his mouth like some devil costumes at Halloween. Well, my friend, think again. The Bible describes Satan as a prince and angel of light (2 Corinthians 11:14) who was cast out of heaven (Luke 10:18).

Let's look at a few other descriptions of Satan in Scripture. He is called the adversary of God and man (I Peter 5:8), prince of the power of the air (Ephesians 2:2), god of this world (John 14:30), who works lying wonders (2 Thessalonians 2:9). In character, he is proud (1 Timothy 3:6), powerful (Ephesians 6:12), wicked (1 John 2:13), subtle (2 Corinthians 11:3), deceitful (2 Corinthians 11:14), fierce, and cruel (Luke 8:29).

Satan's great work on this earth is to keep you from reading the Bible and putting your faith in the Lord Jesus Christ. He comes to kill, steal, and destroy all that is good. This includes marriages, families, the innocence of children (his greatest work against kids is child abuse), morality within a nation, clear definition of genders, and so much more.

But when we put our trust in Christ as our personal Savior, He gives us the power and desire to resist Satan. (Romans 16:20, Ephesians 6:16). As the apostle James, writes: "Resist the devil and he will flee from you" (James 4:7).

There is no other weapon so powerful as God's Word, the Bible. So we need to know it well, study it, and use in our daily lives. Satan flees when we use the Bible against him. The Lord Jesus did this when Satan tested him in the wilderness (Matthew 4:1-11) to teach us how to resist the devil with success.

So What Do You Think?

_____

_____

_____

_____

_____

_____

_____

_____

_____

_____

_____

_____

_____

_____

_____

_____

_____

_____

_____

_____

_____

Old Age

"When I am old and gray headed, O God, forsake me not."

—Psalm 71:18

"Cast me not off in the time of old age; forsake me not when my strength fails."

—Psalm 71:9

"For you are my hope, O Lord God; you are my trust from my youth."

—Psalm 71:5

It is wonderful to walk with God from an early age. It is easier to trust in Him while we are young and moldable. Ecclesiastes 12:1 summarizes this so well: "Remember now thy creator in the days of thy youth, while the evil days come not, nor the years draw near, when you will say, I have no pleasure in them."

That said, when we are young, we strive to be somebody. We want to make a name for ourselves. We want to make an impact somewhere, not only in careers and talents, but even in church ministry or in the world. We want to be known.

When we are older, it is easier to serve the Lord and people because we've worked the kinks out of us. The ego has ebbed, and we settle into who we are with all our faults, talents, and achievements. We settle into God's love for us, and people's opinions really don't matter that much anymore. It's a wonderful way to live. Every day becomes a gift from God. Just the fact that my name didn't appear in the obituary column this morning means I'm have a wonderful day.

Be thankful and grateful for what God has done for you in the past and brought you to this day. Remember, Moses started his greatest ministry at the age of eighty!

So What Do You Think?

_____

_____

_____

_____

_____

_____

_____

_____

_____

_____

_____

_____

_____

_____

_____

God Loves You

"For God so loved the world [you] that He gave us His only Son, that whosoever believes in Him, shall not perish but have everlasting life."
—John 3:16

When we love someone, we pull out all the stops to give gifts we really can't afford. We hope the price of our gift will impress our loved one because we believe the price of the gift is proof of our love. It has more value than something less expensive.

The underlying reason for giving gifts is the hope that the person accepting the gift will realize that he or she is loved. That through our love the person will somehow change, become a better person. If the gift is not received, we are crushed and hurt.

Well, God is like that. He gave His very best gift in a very simple way to prove to you and me that we are so loved. That gift was His Son Jesus Christ, who came as a baby in a manger and grew up in subjection to his parents, just like we did. Jesus was willing to prove His love for us by paying the price for our sins on the cross of Calvary. He died a cruel death at the hands of unbelievers and endured the full wrath of God—all so we could have the gift of eternal life and live with Him forever. What a gift! What a Savior!

To receive this gift, all we need to do is accept the fact that we are sinners, believe Jesus died to pay our debt, and make Him our Lord and Savior. But keep in mind that God's gift is personal, so it must be received personally. God didn't just so love the "world." God so loved ME! If I believe in Him, I receive eternal life. Believe in Him, my friend, and find the fullness of life.

So What Do You Think?

_____

_____

_____

_____

_____

_____

_____

_____

_____

_____

_____

_____

_____

_____

_____

_____

_____

_____

_____

Loneliness or Solitude

"God sets the solitary into families."

—Psalm 68:6

"God said, 'It is not good for man to be alone.'"

—Genesis 2:18

There is a difference between loneliness and solitude. Loneliness is something we don't like. We do everything to try to avoid it. We use alcohol, drugs, sex, quick fixes, shopping, forcing relationships, and sometimes even the ultimate escape—suicide. God made us to bond with other people. He even said so in Genesis 2:18: "It is not good for man to be alone."

Yes, loneliness is something we avoid. In contrast, solitude is something we seek and enjoy. This is because we are never truly alone. Even in solitude, we are in God's presence and can rejoice in His love and friendship.

My dear friend, if you are lonely today, remember you are loved by God. Believe it. I have--and it works! As the apostle Paul, who know what it meant to be alone, expressed: "I am accepted in the Beloved" (Ephesians 1:6).

So use your present loneliness as a preparation for something wonderful God is doing in your life, a life of usefulness and fulfillment. He can bring you all the friends you want. But if He doesn't right now, I'm sure it is because He wants you to know that He is enough! So cuddle up with the heavenly Father who loves you. If you are feeling cold spiritually, just snuggle up because Scripture tells our God "is a consuming fire" (Hebrews 12:29). This will warm you up guaranteed!

So What Do You Think?

_____

_____

_____

_____

_____

_____

_____

_____

_____

_____

_____

_____

_____

_____

_____

_____

_____

_____

_____

_____

_____

_____

Tohu Wa Bohu

"The earth was without form, and void."

—Genesis 1:2

In the original Hebrew language, the second verse of the Bible tells us that the earth was *tohu wa-bohu*. This translates into English as "without form and void."

What exactly does that mean? For me, it means there was nothing! But as we read the rest of the first chapter of Genesis, look what God did to change that. In just six days, He created this beautiful world with its mountains, rivers, valleys, flowers, trees, fields to grow food, insects, and animals. Finally on the sixth day, He made his most intricate and beautiful creation—the man and woman. He made it all by speaking the Word of Faith. He made it out of absolutely nothing— *tohu wa-bohu*. And now here we all are enjoying the results of His creation.

My dear reader, does your life seem right now like a bundle of *tohu wa-bohu*. Of no form and void? Think of what God can do with your life. At the moment, it may feel like nothing. But look what He did with creation. Ask God to do something wonderful, and He will get right on with it!

In 2 Corinthians 5:17, we read that when we put our faith in the Lord Jesus Christ, we become new creatures: "Therefore, if anyone is in Christ, he is a new creation; old things have passed away; behold, all things have become new."

God has taken that old formless *tohu wa-bohu* in our lives and transformed us so we can have a whole new beginning. So trust Him who loves you, died for you, and is waiting for you to come to Him.

So What Do You Think?

_____

_____

_____

_____

_____

_____

_____

_____

_____

_____

_____

_____

_____

_____

_____

_____

_____

_____

_____

Two Shortest Verses in the Bible

"Jesus wept."

—John 11:35

"Rejoice evermore."

—I Thessalonians 5:16

Isn't it great that when we put those two verses together, we see a beautiful, encouraging sermon? Jesus not only wept over His creation ruined by the Fall back in the Garden of Eden, but about all the consequences that have resulted from that Fall. He sweated great, agonizing drops of blood on our behalf in the Garden of Gethsemane. He was willing to pay the price to reverse the consequences of the Fall by giving His own life for us on the cross of Calvary.

We can therefore rejoice. The battle has been won, and we are victors with Him. If Jesus gave Himself for us in His death, will He not give us everything else we need in life?

So, dear reader, whatever you are going through right now, look up and trust your loving Savior. Rejoice because you will get through it. You are victorious. Because Jesus wept, we can rejoice evermore. Hallelujah!

So What Do You Think?

_____

_____

_____

_____

_____

_____

_____

_____

_____

_____

_____

_____

_____

_____

_____

_____

_____

_____

_____

_____

_____

You Are So Loved

"As the Father hath loved Me, so have I loved you."

—John 15:9

But, Lord, I cannot feel you near, I cannot pierce the gloom.
The voice of comfort I can't hear within this lonely room.

O wilt Thou come from Thy far throne beyond the thunder's roar
And melt this heart that feels like stone?
Draw near, draw near once more!

Ah, child, why seek both far and wide My presence wearily?
I never yet have left thy side since thou first trusted Me.

But, Lord, I want to feel Thy love caress this heart of pain.
Have I not sinned against Thee? Can You love me again?

Ah, child, to me thou art ever dear wherever I see thy face,
If wandering far in doubts, in fear, or in the Holy Place.

Hast thou a friend who prays for thee? Thou dost not doubt his care.
And yet he did not bleed for thee; thy sins he did not bear.

Ah, rest in this, I still love thee; I cannot love thee more,
For as the Father loves Me, My love on thee I pour.

—Author Unknown

So What Do You Think?

_____

_____

_____

_____

_____

_____

_____

_____

_____

_____

_____

_____

_____

_____

_____

_____

_____

_____

_____

_____

The Star of David

"I am in my Father, and you are in me and I am in you."
—John 14:20

While I was teaching a Jewish Bible study in New Jersey, I tried to find out the meaning of the Star of David. This was especially significant to me because as a young child in Nazi Germany, I had often seen this star on the sleeves of German Jews. But I couldn't find out a specific meaning. Those Jewish acquaintances I asked had no explanation either. The best answer they could give was that it is mystical.

Since I pray about everything in life, I began praying about it. One morning during my devotional time with the Lord, the answer came to me. The Star of David is a spiritual symbol. It is two triangles intersecting, one triangle pointing down intertwining with the other triangle pointing up. As you know, God is a Trinity, meaning three persons in one— Father, Son, and Holy Spirit. Mankind is also a trinity—body, soul, and spirit. The first triangle symbolizes the Holy Trinity reaching down to humanity while the second symbolizes humanity reaching up to God. When these two triangles intersect, they become one. So the Star of David is a visible, tangible symbol of our union with the Lord.

This in turn made me realize that in a beautiful way that the Star of David isn't just a Jewish symbol but a Christian one. Just as the cross, usually thought of as a Christian symbol, is also a Jewish symbol. We see the cross foreshadowed many times in the Old Testament. For instance at Passover, the blood of the sacrificed lamb was placed on the top and on sides of the front door, making the sign of a cross. The pattern of furnishings given by God for the Tabernacle and Temple arranged in the form of a cross. The snake raised up on a pole in the wilderness to save the Israelites from snakebite was also in the form of a cross (Numbers 21:9).

How wonderful that God has placed symbols of our salvation within the Bible and the culture of His chosen people, the Jews.

So What Do You Think?

_____

_____

_____

_____

_____

_____

_____

_____

_____

_____

_____

_____

_____

_____

Rejection

"And she [Mary] laid him in a manger because there was no room for them in the inn."

—Luke 1:7

Our Lord Jesus Christ knows all about rejection. He was born into this world already rejected by His own people. There was room for other guests in the inn, but not for the Savior come to earth. He was rejected in his adult life and in His ministry.

So, dear believer, if you feel rejected by your parents, friends, boss, society, or even your spouse and children, remember that the most important person in this universe spent His first night in a manger stall in a humble stable. Many people in the Bible were rejected by their family, peers, and society, but God still used them in a mighty way. This includes Moses, Joseph, and David.

But above all, it includes the Lord Jesus Christ, who loves you, came for you into this world, died for you, and is coming back for you. There was no room for Jesus and His family in the inn. But does it really matter? God's gift to us was not in the inn, but lying in the manger in the stable. That's where we find life in its fullness anyway. Jesus said, "I am the way, the truth and the life" (John 14:6).

So, dear friend, if you feel you don't fit in, take heart, take courage, and let God mold you into a mighty person of faith and usefulness to the Lord. If there isn't room for you in the inn, God will not leave you out in the cold. He will find you a place where you can live life in its fullness. And remember that the real important Person in your life didn't fit in either. So take courage and look to Jesus who loves you.

So What Do You Think?

_____

_____

_____

_____

_____

_____

_____

_____

_____

_____

_____

_____

_____

_____

_____

_____

_____

_____

_____

_____

_____

_____

Now Faith

"Now faith is the substance of things hoped for the evidence of things not seen."

—Hebrews 11:1

Folks, if it isn't now, it isn't faith! It is just hoping, wishing, or dreaming. "Now" means immediate obedience. Like Abraham when God told him to take his son Isaac to the mountain and offer him up for a burnt offering (Genesis 22). That would have been a good day to sleep late, don't you think? But Abraham immediately packed his bags and went the very next morning. This earned him the title "Father of Faith."

Abraham also believed God's promises that through Isaac all the nations would be blessed, so he figured God would either spare his son or raise him from the dead (Hebrews 11:17-19). He told his servants, "I and the lad will go yonder to worship and come again to you" (v. 5). As he and Isaac were climbing up that mountain with Isaac carrying the wood, Abraham told Isaac, "My son, God will provide Himself a lamb." What faith in God's Word!

And that is what happened. As Abraham bound Isaac on that altar and raised the knife, a voice from heaven said, "Lay not your hand upon the boy...now I know that you fear God because you have not withheld your son from me." What a test!

Why such a tough test for old Abraham? I think it was because Abraham was so hooked on his son that God had taken second place in his life. When he raised his hand with the knife, he became free from the bondage of worshipping that boy.

God them provided a ram caught in the thicket by his horns. How perfect! A burnt sacrifice had to be without blemish as symbol of the

Lamb of God who would die on the cross. Since this ram was caught by his horns, there wouldn't be a scratch on him. Isaac is a type (foreshadowing) of Jesus Christ, who was also obedient to His Father in going the cross as a sacrifice.

So, dear reader, what are you worshiping in the place of God in your life? Be prepared for God to put His finger on it and tell you to give it up by faith. You will then enjoy life even more, When God is on your throne, all is well.

So What Do You Think?

_____

_____

_____

_____

_____

_____

_____

_____

_____

_____

_____

_____

Tower of Babel and Pentecost

"Come, let us go down, and there confound [confuse] their language, that they may not understand one another's speech."

—Genesis 11:7

"And they were all filled with the Holy Spirit and began to speak with other tongues ...and how hear we every man in our own tongue wherein we were born?"

—Acts 2:4-8

In Genesis 11, we see mankind building a tower with the goal of reaching to heaven and so defying God. At this time mankind still spoke one language. Because of their sin of pride in building the tower, God confused their language so they could no longer understand one another. Hundreds of dialects and languages resulted, as we see to this day.

At the coming of the Holy Spirit in Acts 2, we see languages once again united as the crowd heard the gospel each in their own language. As believers in Messiah Jesus, we now have one heart language with each another because the Holy Spirit comes to indwell every believer who makes up the body, temple, and bride of Christ.

All believers now enjoy the unity of the body of Christ. Just like our human body, all the systems and cells work together to form a healthy spiritual body. How wonderful to know Christ in a personal way and have victory in every situation in our lives, hallelujah!

So What Do You Think?

_____

_____

_____

_____

_____

_____

_____

_____

_____

_____

_____

_____

_____

_____

_____

_____

_____

_____

_____

_____

_____

Forgiveness

"Now therefore be not grieved, nor angry with yourselves, that you sold me [into Egypt] for God did send me before you to preserve life."
—Genesis 45:5

God wants all of us to be useful to Him. To be made useful means we will have to go through testing and trials. These may come in the form of friends, loved ones, and family turning against us. But when we are walking with the Lord, nothing really bad can happen to us regardless of what people may try to do to us. God will use it all for our good to mold us and chisel us for His use.

Joseph is a wonderful example of this. His brothers hated him, threw him into a pit, and then sold him into Egypt where he became a slave. And yet Joseph looked at all they'd done in a positive way as coming from the Lord: "that God did send me before you to preserve life."

What a healthy, godly attitude for all of us to take when we are treated badly. Bitterness and an unforgiving spirit are such harmful, useless emotions in our hearts. They bring about no positive growth, whether in us or in the people we hate.

So let go of unforgiveness and move on in faith, trusting that God may use these toxic people in your life to mold you just as in Joseph's life. Look at the result of Joseph's trials. He became second-in-command of Egypt and helped save from starvation the very family members who had sold him into Egypt. Though they had meant it for evil, God had used it all for good. What an example for us!

So What Do You Think?

_____

_____

_____

_____

_____

_____

_____

_____

_____

_____

_____

_____

_____

_____

_____

_____

_____

_____

_____

_____

Testimony

"God did test Abraham."

—Genesis 22:1

"There he tested them."

—Exodus 15:25

Abraham was tested by the Lord to see if he loved God more than his son. He passed the test: "Now I know that you [Abraham] fear God" (Genesis 22:12). Job also passed a test when he maintained his faith in God even after God allowed Satan to take all his wealth and children (Job 1). Job testified in the midst of his loss, "when He [God] has tried me, I shall come forth as gold" (Genesis 22:12).

Like Job and Abraham, we need to be tested in order to have a testimony. The testing may take months or years. But the end result is that we will become an instrument ready to be used by the Lord. God is ruthless when it comes to training us. But we know that His loving hands will not test us beyond what we are able to endure (1 Corinthians 10:13).

So, my friend, be assured that if you want to have a testimony for the Lord, you will need to be tested. As well-known Bible teacher Joyce Myer once said, "If you are never tested, you don't have a testimony. You will only have a MONY."

So What Do You Think?

_____

_____

_____

_____

_____

_____

_____

_____

_____

_____

_____

_____

_____

_____

_____

_____

_____

_____

_____

_____

My Bible

Hello, I'm your Bible. Don't keep me on the shelf!
I can teach you all so many things about yourself.

When I'm opened up and read, I have so much to give
I can share the love of God and show you how to live.

But God expected good things from us, so I must share that too
Because He made you, He knows what is best for you.

So pick me up and dust me off. I am a special Book.
Step into my pages now — come take a closer look!

I am the door to LIFE!

The Bible has been the world's bestseller for centuries. Dictators have burned it, denied it, and ridiculed the people who believe it. But the Bible has endured the test of time. Satan, man's great enemy, hates it and will do everything to keep you from it.

So, my friend, make it your daily guidebook. You will never fail.

So What Do You Think?

The Napkin Undisturbed

> Then Simon Peter came, following him, and went into the tomb; and he saw the linen cloths lying *there,* and the handkerchief[napkin] that had been around His head, not lying with the linen cloths, but folded together in a place by itself [undisturbed].
>
> —John 20:6-7

When the Lord Jesus Christ rose from the dead, His burial shroud was undisturbed. Why? Because in His new resurrected body, Jesus could walk right through walls—or linen wrappings—and wasn't confined by physical matter (Luke 24:36-43).

I suddenly remembered this verse one evening in New York City. My husband used to take me to many very elegant restaurants there. When a couple dined at this particular restaurant, only the man's menu had the price list. The menu given to the woman didn't show any prices so as not to concern her about cost.

What impressed me most was how artistically folded the napkin was at each place setting. I used to study the many folds before I opened my napkin. If I left the table during dinner to powder my nose, the waiter would refold the napkin during my absence exactly into its original shape. Why? Because he knew I was coming back. When I returned, the napkin looked as undisturbed as though I'd never opened it.

In the same way, the undisturbed folds of Jesus's burial wrappings is a reminder that our Lord is coming back—and sooner than we may think.

So What Do You Think?

_____

_____

_____

_____

_____

_____

_____

_____

_____

_____

_____

_____

_____

_____

_____

_____

_____

_____

_____

_____

_____

_____

How Rich We Are!

All the blessings in the first chapter of Ephesians are in the past tense. Notice how many time past tense verbs are used, especially past-perfect verbs like "has" and "have" or "having." God has already made these blessings ours from the moment we open our hearts to the Lord Jesus Christ. Notice also the little word "in." These blessings are ours to enjoy only *in* Christ.

"Blessed *be* the God and Father of our Lord Jesus Christ, who **has** blessed us with every spiritual blessing **in** the heavenly *places* in Christ, just as He **chose** us **in** Him before the foundation of the world . . . **having** predestined us to adoption as sons by Jesus Christ to Himself, according to the good pleasure of His will, to the praise of the glory of His grace, by which He **made** us accepted **in** the Beloved. **In** Him we **have** redemption through His blood, the forgiveness of sins, according to the riches of His grace which He **made** to abound toward us **in** all wisdom and prudence, **having** made known to us the mystery of His will . . . that in the dispensation of the fullness of the times He might gather together in one all things **in** Christ, both which are in heaven and which are on earth—**in** Him. **In** Him also we **have** obtained an inheritance . . . **In** Him you also trusted, after you heard the word of truth, the gospel of your salvation; **in** whom also, having believed, you **were** sealed with the Holy Spirit of promise."

—Ephesians 1:3-13

So, my friend, you are rich. Enjoy all of your wonderful inheritance. But this is possible only by faith. So let's make Jesus Christ our Lord and Savior today and take all these promises into our hearts and lives. And let's give Him thanks today because He is for us!

So What Do You Think?

Satan, "god" of this World

Adam was manager, boss, or "god" of this world:

"And the Lord God took the man and put him into the garden of Eden to till it and to keep it...and whatsoever Adam called every living creature, that was the name thereof."

—Genesis 2:15-19

Jesus used the Bible and won the battle:

"And the devil, taking him [Jesus] up into a high mountain, showed him all the kingdoms of the world in a moment of time...saying..."all this authority will I give you and the glory of them; if you worship me." Jesus said..."Get thee behind me Satan."

—Luke 4:5-8

If our gospel be hid, it is hid to them that are lost; in whom the god of this world [Satan] has blinded the minds of them which believe not, lest the light of the glorious gospel of Christ, who is the image of God, should shine unto them.

—2 Corinthians 4:4

Who does Satan think he is? The Lord God put Adam in charge of this world. So how did Satan get to be the "god" of this world and have all this authority?

Adam gave it to him in the Garden of Eden when he sinned against the command of God. He committed high treason and so lost the position God had given him. Satan took over, and what a mess he has made ever since!

"So God drove out the man from the Garden of Eden and he placed cherubim at the east of the garden and a flaming sword which turned every way, to guard the way of the tree of life."

—Genesis 3:23

So, my friend, if you blame God for all the mess we are in, remember these Bible verses. Satan is the "god" of this world, and Adam gave this authority to him. Satan hates God, you and me, and especially children. If he can get children abused early in life, he will most often have that person their entire life, either by continued abuse and thinking it is okay or living into adulthood with a victim mentality.

How can we resist Satan? By wearing the armor of God (Ephesians 6:10-17) and by knowing the Bible, which is the sword of the Spirit (Ephesians 6:17, Hebrews 4:12), well and using it against Satan just as Jesus Christ showed us during His temptation in the wilderness.

So What Do You Think?

_____

_____

_____

_____

_____

_____

_____

_____

_____

Part Two:

Meditations to Help You Think

For he shall be like a tree planted by the waters,
Which spreads out its roots by the river,
And will not fear when heat comes;
But its leaf will be green,
And will not be anxious in the year of drought,
Nor will cease from yielding fruit.
—Jeremiah 17:8

The Snake Talked

"Now the serpent was more subtle than any beast of the field and he said unto the woman, 'yea, hath God said' if you eat of the tree of the knowledge of good and evil you will die ?... and the serpent said unto the woman, 'ye shall not surely die'..."

—Genesis 3:1-4

This conversation between Satan (who indwelt the snake) and Eve is very interesting. Please read the complete account in the third chapter of Genesis. What jumps out at me in this story is that Eve wasn't surprised, frightened, or shocked that the snake had a voice. Why didn't she question the fact that this snake was carrying on an intelligent conversation with her, trying to make her doubt God?

Could it be that perhaps all animals had a voice before the Fall? Perhaps the animals communed not only with Adam and Eve but with each other. Then it would seem logical for Eve to listen to this dialogue.

The point in this text isn't what kind of fruit Eve ate but the fact that she and Adam disobeyed God's command of God. This is called "sin." Though such a small three-letter word, it has affected all of humanity and the world. Satan is a great deceiver. He makes sin look good, but he never tells us of the consequences.

Could this passage mean then that all the animals lost their voices after Adam and Eve sinned? I don't know, but it is an interesting thought. We read in Romans 8:22 that "the whole creation groans and travails in pain." Joel 1:18 describes "how the beasts groan." Just something to think about!

So What Do You Think?

_____

_____

_____

_____

_____

_____

_____

_____

_____

_____

_____

_____

_____

_____

_____

_____

_____

_____

_____

_____

_____

The Christian Life

"For the wages of sin is death, but the gift of God is eternal life, through Jesus Christ our Lord."

—Romans 6:23

The Christian life is a gift from God. Jesus Christ paid the price for our redemption when He died for our sins on the cross of Calvary. We become Christians when we put our faith and trust in this wonderful finished work. This is not automatic. It is a choice we have to make. Just like sitting in your garage doesn't make you a car, so sitting in a church pew doesn't make you a Christian. You will just warm the pew.

Just like getting married, there should be a day, a time, and a place when you make the decision to have eternal life. There was a day, a time, and a place when I said to my husband Bob, "I take you to be my wedded husband to have and to hold from this day forward."

So it is with becoming a Christian. For me it was Thursday, February 25, 1954 at 8:45 a.m. . That was more than sixty-five years ago, and the bubbles still haven't worn off!

So What Do You Think?

_____

_____

_____

_____

_____

_____

_____

_____

_____

_____

_____

_____

_____

_____

_____

_____

_____

_____

_____

_____

Friends versus Enemies

"That we should no longer be children...but, speaking the truth in love, may grow up in all things into Him who is the head—Christ."
—Ephesians 4:14-15

To have wonderful friends enriches our lives. We can't have enough of them. They encourage us, accept us as we are, and we value their opinions in our decision-making process. But friends can only lead us to the edge of success whereas our enemies can actually spur us on to greater heights and accomplishments.

David, the son of Jesse, is a perfect example. When the prophet Samuel came to Jesse's house to anoint one of his sons, Jesse brought out his seven sons, excluding the youngest, David. When we read between the lines, we see he was probably not considered worthy by his dad. He was rejected at home, not only by his father Jesse but his older brothers.

Samuel looked at all the handsome young men in front of him, but none was the one chosen by God. He asked if there was another son. So Jesse brought in David, who was outside caring for the sheep. Samuel then anointed David as the next king of Israel in front of the whole family, who were probably very surprised by it all.

God chooses people who are rejected by their family. Many very successful people have had to face rejection before achieving great heights of success. The fact that David was anointed king of Israel didn't mean much to him at the time. He didn't go out shopping for crowns but right back out to care for the sheep.

But when Goliath threatened the armies of Israel, David rose to the occasion, spoke to Goliath in the power of the Lord, and won the victory that day over his enemy. It was when the enemy challenged him that David realized that he was God's anointed king and had the authority to speak like one.

So it is in our lives. If we don't confront the giants in our past, we will continue living every day with a victim mentality, letting the voices within us from the past judge and condemn us. But as a Christian, we have the authority to confront any enemy that challenges us in the Name of the Lord. When we speak the truth in love, we actually grow up into Christ in all things.

So, my friend, if you need to confront someone in your life who has abused, belittled, abandoned, or neglected you, confront them as an adult (Ephesians 4:15). You will be surprised how you will "grow up" in other things as well.

So What Do You Think?

_____

_____

_____

_____

_____

_____

_____

_____

_____

_____

_____

I Will Trust

"I trust in the LORD."

—Psalm 31:6

"Whenever I am afraid, I will trust in You."

—Psalm 56:3

It is interesting to read through the book of Psalms and see how many times we read the words "I trust" or "I have put my trust" or "I will trust." King David and the other psalmists struggled with difficult doubts, problems, and situations just as we do. Their feelings were not always filled with faith.

But they decided then and there that it isn't by feelings that we trust and serve the Lord. It is a choice. It is by our will.

So, my friend, if you struggle with doubts, remember it is when you make up your mind to trust the Lord that you will be on your way to a life of peace and victory in your walk with the Lord.

So What Do You Think?

_____

_____

_____

_____

_____

_____

_____

_____

_____

_____

_____

_____

_____

_____

_____

_____

_____

_____

_____

_____

Ups and Downs in Life

The ups and downs in life prove we are alive just as when a hospital patient is hooked up to a heart monitor. So long as the cardiogram shows the normal up and down lines of a steady heartbeat, the doctors and nurses know all is well. But when the monitor suddenly displays no more ups and downs, just a flat line, medical staff and equipment gets rushed into the room to try to revive the patient. If that straight line continues, it means the patient is dead.

So, my dear friend, if your life is filled with ups and downs, be thankful. It shows that you are alive!

Now if you are feeling a constant underlying emptiness, loneliness, and uselessness, maybe it's time for you to focus on the words of Jesus in John10:10: "I came to give you life and that more abundantly."

If your life doesn't feel abundant, the answer may be to double up on your private time with the Lord. Find a quiet place once a day and make it a spiritual sanctuary to let the Lord speak to your heart and read some of the loving promises God has put into the Bible for you. One of my favorites is Psalm 91:1: "He who dwells in the Secret Place of the most High shall abide under the shadow of the Almighty."

So What Do You Think?

_____

_____

_____

_____

_____

_____

_____

_____

_____

_____

_____

_____

_____

_____

_____

_____

_____

_____

_____

_____

Pikes Peak

"How shall they call on him in whom they have not believed? And how shall they believe in him of whom they have not heard? And how shall they hear without a preacher?...So then faith comes by hearing, and hearing by the word of God."

—Romans 10:14-17

Some Christian denominations feel we don't really need to preach the gospel because God has already predestined, selected, and chosen which people will become believers and part of the body of Christ. I have a problem with this theology! The words of Jesus were very clear: "Go into all the world and preach the gospel to every creature" (Matthew 28:19).

Other Christians will say that nature is a witness so people don't need to hear the Word of God. What nonsense! No one ever got saved staring at Pikes Peak. It is when the Word of God is preached that the Holy Spirit can quicken the heart to believe. As the apostle Paul told the Roman church in the above passage, faith comes by hearing the Word of God.

Let's face it! God has no physical hands, feet, or mouth on this earth. He needs ours. He uses ours. So let's get the Good News out to a very dark and dying world.

So What Do You Think?

_____

_____

_____

_____

_____

_____

_____

_____

_____

_____

_____

_____

_____

_____

_____

_____

_____

_____

_____

Serving Their Own Gods

"They feared the Lord, yet served their own gods."

—2 Kings 17:33

What kind of a verse is this? How can this be true of God's people, the Israelites, whom He had rescued from slavery in Egypt?

Sadly, it's easy. So let's not be too critical of the Israelites. We do the same thing in our daily lives when we fear and respect the Lord on Sundays but serve our own gods the rest of the time. What are our priorities in life? Do we really think about eternity? Remember, all the things we worry about today won't matter a hundred years from now.

It's healthy to examine our hearts and lives to make sure we are on track with the Lord's purpose for us and destiny for our lives. How can we do this? By being in the Word regularly. Not just reading and absorbing it, but also to giving it out to others. Christians grow spiritually when they give out the gospel, whether by teaching a formal Bible class or just sharing the gospel in conversation.

So What Do You Think?

_____

_____

_____

_____

_____

_____

_____

_____

_____

_____

_____

_____

_____

_____

_____

_____

_____

_____

_____

_____

_____

_____

The Book of Job

"So the Lord blessed the latter end of Job more than his beginning."
—Job 42:12

For me, the best way to read the book of Job is to begin with the last chapter, which tells us that the Lord gave Job twice as much as he had before and blessed Job's latter end more than his beginning.

Why begin with the last chapter? Because the first chapter makes a lot more sense that way. Job had to be tested by the Lord before he was able to handle all the blessings God had prepared for him in the last chapter. We also see that Satan tried to shake his faith and make him curse God. In fact, he used the mouth of Job's wife to tell him to curse God and die.

So, my friend, are you going through the fire right now? Remember, your great enemy is at work with God's permission to strip you to make you ready to receive a great blessing also. Job's words that we read in the book of Job are filled with faith even in the middle of his suffering when he didn't understand what was happening:

"Acquaint now thyself with Him and be at peace, thereby good shall come unto you."   —Job 22:21

"But He knows the way that I take, when He has tried [tested] me, I shall come forth as gold...I have esteemed the words of His mouth [the Bible] more than my necessary food...for He performs the thing that is appointed for me."
—Job 23:10- 14

What a man of faith and courage! How encouraged we can all be to have the full Word of God in our hands. Let's study it, meditate on it, digest it, memorize it, and give it out.

So What Do You Think?

_____

_____

_____

_____

_____

_____

_____

_____

_____

_____

_____

_____

_____

_____

_____

_____

_____

_____

_____

_____

Your Local Church

No one can rise higher spiritually in their walk with God than the spirituality of their local church. If you are not being fed and challenged, it is probably time for you to pray about finding another church. God will lead you.

This isn't an easy task. But if you want to grow in the Lord and serve Him, you need to be fed, encouraged, and spiritually supported by the church you attend.

You will be surprised how God will bless you, opening new doors of friendship and growth for you, once you make the move.

So What Do You Think?

_____

_____

_____

_____

_____

_____

_____

_____

_____

_____

_____

_____

_____

_____

_____

_____

_____

_____

_____

_____

_____

_____

_____

_____

Created and Formed

"But now thus saith the Lord, who created you, O Jacob, and he who formed you, O Israel, fear not; for I have redeemed you, I have called you by your name, you are mine. When you pass through the waters, I will be with you, and through the rivers, they shall not overflow you, when you walk through the fire, you shall not be burned, neither shall the flame kindle upon you."

—Isaiah 43:1-2

Jacob is the human name of Abraham's grandson, whose twelve sons became the twelve tribes of Israel. We see his old human nature in full color in the book of Genesis. He was a liar, a cheat, and a deceiver. But God had His hand on Jacob's life.

The above passages tells us that God "formed" Jacob into Israel, meaning "a prince with God." This shows that God was personally involved in shaping Jacob into a spiritual man just as though God used His hands to form Jacob. How did God do that, and what methods did He use to bring this about? The answer is in the second verse above. It was the waters, the rivers, and the fire.

So, my dear reader, take courage and know that all the trials, pain, loneliness, and hurts that come into your life are God's tools to mold you, shape you, and force you to trust the loving hands of God. They are sent to make you a spiritually strong believer. Focus on God's love for you and thank him for it all.

The very next verse in this passage assures us: "Since you are precious in my sight, you have been honorable and I [God] have loved you" (Isaiah 43:4).

You are loved by God. You are never alone. God is always with you. So trust Him!

So What Do You Think?

_____

_____

_____

_____

_____

_____

_____

_____

_____

_____

_____

_____

_____

_____

_____

_____

_____

_____

_____

Treasures of Darkness

"And I will give you the treasures of darkness, and hidden riches of secret places, that you may know that I, the Lord, who called you by your name am the God of Israel."

—Isaiah 45:3

Humanly speaking, we don't think of darkness as having any kind of treasure in it. In fact, the electric light bulb was invented to prolong the daylight. But here we read that there are treasures in darkness. Not only in nature, when vegetation goes into some kind of rest, but also in our lives. Darkness is an important part of growth for plants, animals, and mankind. During sleep, for example, our brain cells renew themselves and all the systems of our body detox into the colon to be eliminated. If that isn't happening in the human body, illness will result.

In Psalm 139 we read that we are "fearfully and wonderfully made." In fact, God created our bodies so that they are able to heal themselves. What a God we have to create such an intricate body! So we must take good care of it. But how? Here are just a few tips that have worked for me.

- After the age of fifty, take digestive enzymes and probiotics with every meal.
- Eat smaller meals more often throughout the day.
- Walk at least a half -hour each day and even twice a day.
- Drink a large glass of water upon getting out of bed.
- Eat less red meat and more fish, beans, and vegetables.
- Go easy on sweets.
- Don't eat or drink after 7:00 pm.

- Most importantly, begin and end your day with the Lord, including Bible reading and prayer.

I've done all of these for over thirty years and have more energy now than when I was thirty years old!

So What Do You Think?

_____

_____

_____

_____

_____

_____

_____

_____

_____

_____

_____

_____

_____

_____

The God Who Hides Himself

"Verily You are a God who hides Yourself, O God of Israel, the Savior.

—Isaiah 45:15

"Those that seek Me early shall find Me."

—Proverbs 8:17

"You shall seek Me and find Me."

—Jeremiah 29:13

"The Lord is good to the soul that seeks Him."

—Lamentations 3:25

Isn't it wonderful that God hides Himself so that He can be easily found? How do we find someone who is invisible and intangible? We can only do this by believing the Bible promises and living by what they say. Peace in your heart will result.

This becomes easier as one gets older. When you have walked with God for many years, many of the Bible promises will have become a part of your life. When trials come, your mind and heart can instantly rely on one or more promises you have stored in your heart. This will help you to keep going.

Make it a daily challenge to memorize Scripture. Someday the Bible may become a forbidden book to read. Most dictators of this world have done this! So take the opportunity to hide it in your heart while you still have the freedom to do so.

So What Do You Think?

_____

_____

_____

_____

_____

_____

_____

_____

_____

_____

_____

_____

_____

_____

_____

_____

_____

_____

_____

_____

_____

_____

Alone Again

"God relieves the fatherless and the widow."

—Psalm 146:9

"Let thy widows trust in me."

—Jeremiah 49:11

According to psychologists, widowhood is at the top of the list for stress. Yet sooner or later, if you are in a close relationship, one of you will go first and the one left will be in widowhood.

God has promised throughout the Bible that he takes special care of widows. I have experienced this in a very wonderful way. I make everything spiritual, including my widowhood. I look at it as a "God Thing." My husband's work on this earth was done, so he went home to heaven. Mine isn't done so I am still here. I am busier now serving the Lord than I ever was while I was married. Yes, there are lonely moments, but I don't stay there. I double up on my time in my Bible and encourage myself in God's love for me and how He has planned my life.

So widowhood is a new life, only different! After having grieved three months after my husband's death from September 1993 to January 1, 1994, I decided to move all the furniture around. I moved the bed to the other side of the room. I moved my husband's favorite chair into another room and threw out his toothbrushes and combs. I was crying as I did it, but this was the only way to move forward.

Slowly, I became a new woman with a new life, new goals, and lots of activities helping people. I realized that misery in widowhood is natural, but a positive attitude is a choice. I forced myself to do this, and it worked. Interestingly enough, other widows began coming to me for encouragement when they saw what I did with my life.

My grieving friend, God understands. But He also has some work for you to do as a single in a world of twos. God removed your mate to have you all to Himself, to love, embrace, bless, and use you to help others. He has done this for me.

Remember, many of the great people in the Bible and throughout history have been alone. It was during their lonely times that great inventions, ideas, and world-changing things came into being.

So it will be for you, my friend. A whole new life is ahead of you, and some wonderful things will open up to you. In fact, your greatest work may still be up ahead.

So What Do You Think?

Fear Not

"Fear not; for I am with you. Be not dismayed; for I am thy God, I will strengthen you, yes, I will help you, yea, I will uphold you with my right hand of my righteousness."

—Isaiah 41:10-13

There are 366 "fear nots" in the Bible. That means one for every day of the year, including Leap Year!

God understands our fears. They are the result of man's Fall in the Garden of Eden. We fear the unknown. We fear old age and death. Scientists have determined that we are born with just two fears—the fear of noise and the fear of falling—and that all other fears are learned. This means we can unlearn them.

We often think the opposite of fear is courage . But in fact, the opposite of fear is love, as the apostle John explains: "God is love. Whoever lives in love lives in God, and God in them…There is no fear in love. But perfect love drives out fear, because fear has to do with punishment" (1 John 4:16,18).

When we know we are loved, we feel secure. Believe the love God has for you, and fear will take flight out of your life. Here are a few more Bible verses to remind us that we need not fear.

"God gives you rest from fear."

—Isaiah 14:3

"My heart shall not fear."

—Psalm 27:3

"I will trust and not be afraid."

—Isaiah 12:2

So, dear friend, when fear knocks at your door, don't put on the coffee! Choose faith, not fear. It is a matter of the will.

So What Do You Think?

_____

_____

_____

_____

_____

_____

_____

_____

_____

_____

_____

_____

_____

_____

_____

_____

_____

_____

Women Really Rule This World

"Now the snake was more subtle than any beast of the field which the Lord God had made. And he said unto the woman, Yes, hath God said, you shall not eat of every tree of the garden? Yes, said the woman, but of the fruit of the tree which is in the middle of the garden, God said, you shall not eat of it, you will die.' Satan said...you shall not surely die!' And when the woman saw that the tree was good for food, pleasant to the eyes, and a tree to make one wise, she took of the fruit and did eat, and gave also to her husband with her, and he did eat.

—Genesis 3:1-6

It all started in the Garden of Eden. Satan deceived Eve, not Adam, because he knew Eve was the real boss. Getting her to disobey God was the way to get Adam as well. Women throughout history have influenced not only men but nations as well. Here are some examples from the Bible.

Eve influenced Adam (Genesis 3). Sarah influenced Abraham to take Hagar (Genesis 16). Rebecca influenced her son Jacob to deceive Isaac, his father (Genesis 27). Abigail influenced David not to kill her husband (I Samuel 25). And many more.

It has been said that "the hand that rocks the cradle rules the world." Are you a friend to your husband, or do you tear him down? Do you nurture him, or are you in competition with him? Men many times do look to women to guide them (but of course we'll never tell them that, right???).

So What Do You Think?

_____

_____

_____

_____

_____

_____

_____

_____

_____

_____

_____

_____

_____

_____

_____

_____

_____

_____

_____

_____

Walking in the Spirit

"It is the Spirit that gives life….the words that I speak unto you, they are Spirit and they are life."

—John 6:63

"But the fruit [let's make sure it is always "fresh fruit"!] of the Spirit is love, joy, peace, long-suffering [patience], gentleness, goodness and faith, meekness and self-control, against such there is no law."

—Galatians 5:22-23

"For the law of the Spirit of life in Christ Jesus has [past tense] made me free from the law of sin and death."

—Romans 8:2

What does it mean to walk in the Spirit? How do we do this? Does it mean that I am to pray, work, speak, and at the same time be constantly thinking about the Lord or a Bible verse?

No, I don't think it means that. To me, walking in the Spirit simply means believing and living by the words the Lord Jesus Christ said in the Word of God, the Bible.

When the Bible talks about the law, it is like the law of gravity. It works whether I believe it or not. The law of sin is death. Death happens, whether I believe it or not!

So is living in the Spirit of God. When we have accepted the words of the Bible that we have sinned, that Jesus Christ paid the penalty for sin on the cross of Calvary, and that He rose again from the dead all for us, then the Holy Spirit of God comes to live inside of us, never to leave us or forsake us (Hebrews 13:5). It is a law, like gravity. I can totally believe it, rest on it, and live accordingly every day.

How blessed we are to know this truth. I have become a container of the Holy Spirit of God, and the words of Jesus Christ are my guide for living. The Spirit leads, loves, and guides me. I can rest assured this is true. It is a law—the law of the Spirit of life (Romans 8:2)—that is always in operation of our lives.

So, my friend, focus on this truth and you will have an easier time in your daily life. Laws work, and so will this!

So What Do You Think?

_____

_____

_____

_____

_____

_____

_____

_____

_____

_____

_____

_____

Abide in Me and I in You

"Abide in me and I in you. As the branch cannot bear fruit of itself, except it abide in the vine, no more can you, except you abide in me. I am the vine, and you are the branches. He that abides in me, and I in him, the same brings forth much fruit....for without me you can do nothing'...If you abide in me, and my words abide in you, you shall ask what you will, and it shall be done unto you. In this is my Father glorified that you bear much fruit, so shall you be my disciples. As the Father has loved me so have I loved you; continue you in my love."

—John 15:4-9

In these verses, our Lord Jesus Christ tells us how to live a very productive, peaceful, and useful life. It is very simple. Just abide like a branch abides on a tree. No struggle. No wondering if God is using you. No questioning your purpose in life. Just be close to Jesus. "Hang out" with your Lord and Savior.

Again, it is a focus within you. Meditate on a verse. Maybe memorize some portions of Scripture. Or just let the Lord love you. It's really that simple!

So What Do You Think?

God Uses Women to Change the World

It's interesting that when God has wanted to change the course of history, He has often used a woman. Among women God has used to impact history for the good was **Susan B. Anthony**, who fought for women's suffrage as well as to end slavery. She saw the end of slavery, but didn't live to see the nineteenth amendment ratified in 1920, which was named the Susan B. Anthony Amendment.

Dr. Elizabeth Blackwell was the first woman to receive a medical degree from an all-male American medical school. She opened the New York Infirmary for Women and Children in 1856. **Marie Curie** was the first woman professor of General Physics in the Faculty of Sciences at the Sorbonne in Paris in 1906 and the first person to win two Nobel Prizes in the study of spontaneous radiation. **Mother Theresa**, a Catholic nun, founded the Order of Missionaries of Charity and was awarded the Nobel Peace Prize for her work against poverty in India.

More recently, **Rosa Parks** was named the First Lady of Civil Rights for her role in the civil rights movement when she refused to give up her bus seat to a white man. **Ellen Johnson-Sirleaf** became the first elected female head of state in Africa when she took office president of Liberia in January 2006. She and two other female leaders were awarded the 2011 Nobel Peace Prize for their nonviolent role in promoting peace, democracy and gender equality.

Sadly, Satan is a copycat and tries to do what God does. So he too has used women in his scheme to destroy the world. **Madeline O'Hare** is just one such. She founded the Atheist Society and went to the Supreme Court to get the Bible and prayer out of public schools.

So What Do You Think?

_____

_____

_____

_____

_____

_____

_____

_____

_____

_____

_____

_____

_____

_____

_____

_____

_____

_____

_____

_____

_____

_____

God is a Romantic

"His left hand is under my head, and His right hand embraces me."
—Song of Solomon 2:6

"You are all fair, my love, there is no spot in you."
—Song of Solomon 4:7

"Your Maker is your husband."
—Isaiah 54:5

God holds you constantly in a never-ending close embrace. Believe it! You are loved, held, and cherished by the One who made you. Rejoice in it and live accordingly!

Living with the realization that you are so loved will actually help you enjoy other people more, especially a mate. You will be able to take the pressure off your husband, family members, and friends. You will no longer have expectations of them to make you happy every minute. Husbands can't do that, and friends may not really know your needs. A smart wife will get her deep need for love from the Lord, her eternal and spiritual husband.

And what a husband God is! I know. I've been widowed now for over twenty-five years, and God's love becomes more precious with each passing year. Once this wonderful truth really grips you, you will flourish in your devotions and in your service to God and others. You will be settled in God's love for you, and the opinions of others really won't matter that much anymore.

So, my dear friend, receive the love God has for you. It will change your life from now on.

So What Do You Think?

_____

_____

_____

_____

_____

_____

_____

_____

_____

_____

_____

_____

_____

_____

_____

_____

_____

_____

_____

Power to Become Sons

"He came unto His own [the Jewish people] and His own received him not. But as many as received Him, to them gave He power to become sons, even to them that believe on His name."

—John 1:12

As we see in the verse above, God gives us the power to become sons. But some people remain children forever in all they do. If we want to grow up, a choice needs to be made.

So what is the difference between a child and a son? We rarely see signs that proclaim, "Jake and Child Contractors." No, we see "Jake and Son Contractors." The son has grown up, and father and son are working together in harmony to achieve what is best for the company.

So it is in spiritual things. When we have matured a bit in our faith, we are in alignment with God's will. We think like God in our service. We are able to love and serve people like He does. Growing up may be a natural thing for a child in a family. But in spiritual things, it is a choice. God gives us the power to become grownup sons, not children. So let's move forward and grow up into Him in all things.

So What Do You Think?

Spiritual Constipation

What exactly is spiritual constipation? Is that even possible? How can that be? It is very simple. Spiritual constipation means we are forever taking in and never giving out.

We take in truths, Scripture, encouragements, people's answered prayers, and testimonies from other Christians who have achieved great accomplishments for God. We are forever running to as many Bible studies as possible along with our weekly church sermons. Or Bible conferences and spiritual "how-to" seminars. Plus we devour the countless devotional periodicals, Christian publications, and inspirational websites that are available.

But how does this make us "constipated" spiritually? If the digestive system is not functioning properly, the body will eventually break down. Similarly, if we only take things into our lives and never give them out, we become stagnant in our spiritual life. Our Lord Jesus commanded us to "go into all the world and preach the Gospel to every creature" (Mark 16:15), not to simply sit at the spiritual table and gorge ourselves.

I am over eighty years old and have taught Bible classes for close to fifty years. I am also involved with many children's ministries. I mentor young people and the elderly as well as do marriage counseling. I average seventy speaking engagements per year. I have authored one book and am currently writing two more. If I can do it, so can you!

So, my friend, let's get healthy spiritually and take in blessings but also give them out. How can you do this? You can pick up the phone and encourage a troubled person with a Bible verse or a prayer. Better yet, begin to visit people and pray with them. You can pass on whatever you hear or read from God's Word. You will be the one who is blessed more than the people receiving your encouraging words.

So What Do You Think?

_____

_____

_____

_____

_____

_____

_____

_____

_____

_____

_____

_____

_____

_____

_____

_____

_____

_____

The Old Testament is a Latticework

"My beloved is like a roe or a young hart; behold he stands behind our wall, he looks forth at the windows, showing himself through the lattice."

—Song of Solomon 2:9

Latticework is a decorative framework consisting of a crisscrossed pattern of strips, whether made of wood, metal, or even stone. What is significant about a lattice is that you can see through it but not clearly. The openings in the lattice only give glimpses of what is on the other side. We don't see the whole thing. So it is with Messiah in the Old Testament. The biblical stories foretell of Jesus Christ but only as a shadow. For example:

- Joseph's life is a perfect foreshadowing of the life of Jesus Christ (Genesis 37 to 50).
- Isaac is a shadow of Jesus Christ's willingness to die in obedience (Genesis 22).
- Moses leading Israel out of bondage foreshadows Christ leading people into spiritual freedom (Exodus).
- The bronze snake lifted up on a pole in the wilderness to heal those who looked foreshadowed Christ on the cross (Numbers 21).
- The blood of the Passover lamb on the doorposts was in the shape of a cross (Exodus 12).
- The furniture in the tabernacle was arranged in the shape of a cross (Exodus 25-28).
- Psalm 22 describes in detail the death and resurrection of the Messiah ,Jesus Christ.
- Isaiah 53 also describes the suffering of Messiah.

Connecting the Old Testament with the New Testament is a wonderful way to study the Bible because the Old and New Testaments are really one single book. As the saying goes, "the Old Testament is in the New Testament revealed, and the New Testament is in the Old Testament concealed."

So What Do You Think?

_____

_____

_____

_____

_____

_____

_____

_____

_____

_____

_____

_____

_____

Ebb and Flow

Just as the ocean has an ebb and flow, so do our lives. Spending some time at the beach is so refreshing, not only to watch the tide come in and go out, but the soothing sound of it all.

So what happens when the tide is out? There is a dryness on the beach. All the debris has landed. The seagulls pick through the sand to find some food. There are actual holes in the sand and an emptiness.

So it is in our lives. We think we are in the Lord's will, but nothing much is happening. We faithfully spend time in God's Word and serve. But we see no answers to prayer and begin to wonder.

But this is a necessary time in our lives. It is a time to look within. To clean up the debris that has risen to the top. To know that God loves you. No big "aha" moments, just the usual daily routine. This is also the best time to double up on our time with the Lord. The reason He wants you to get that debris up and out is because He is looking for clean vessels to use for future use.

Remember Joseph (Genesis 37- 50). Look how many years the tide was out for him, both as a slave and then for thirteen years in jail. But God used those thirteen dry years to prepare Joseph for the job God had in store for him as leader of Egypt.

So, my friend, if the tide is out right now in your life, just wait and see how very full the tide will be when it comes back into your life.

So What Do You Think?

_____

_____

_____

_____

_____

_____

_____

_____

_____

_____

_____

_____

_____

_____

_____

_____

_____

_____

_____

_____

_____

_____

Hunger and Thirst

"I am the Bread of Life."

—John 6:35

"I am the Living Water."

—John 7:37-39

Our Lord Jesus Christ, who is the Bread of Life, began His ministry being hungry. He who said, "I am the Living Water" ended His earthly life being thirsty. He purposely did all this for us so that you and I never need to be hungry or thirsty. What a wonderful Savior we have!

Notice that Jesus used symbols in describing Himself that would be understood in all areas of the world as well as all time periods throughout history. He didn't call Himself some kind of fancy croissant or other pastry. He didn't reference sparkling champagne or bubbling Perrier mineral water. He uses simple examples that everyone in every culture would understand.

Just plain bread (or at least some form of carbohydrate, whether made of wheat as in Israel of Jesus's day or made of rice or corn in Asia or the Americas) and water are vital daily necessities for every person. Without them people would not survive. In describing Himself as the Bread of Life and Living Water, Jesus is saying that we cannot survive apart from Him and that He is the Source to meet all our needs in life if we believe in Him.

So What Do You Think?

Immersion or Sprinkling?

"Repent and be baptized."

—Acts 2:38

"Many . . . believed and were baptized."

—Acts 18:8

This is only my opinion, and if you disagree let's still be friends.

No one is born a Christian. It is a choice we each must make, a vital decision both in life now and for eternity. We become Christians when we receive Jesus Christ into our lives.

Once we have received Jesus, the Bible teaches that being baptized is an outward profession to others of what we have done in our hearts. Some denominations believe that sprinkling a baby serves as baptism. They use the biblical example of baby boys being circumcised at birth. This is a decision made by the parents, not the child. The baby has no idea what is happening.

So if sprinkling is comparable to circumcision, what about baby girls? Are they excluded from this blessing? I don't think so. The Bible teaches that we must first repent and choose to believe. Then baptism is to follow. So sprinkling a baby can't be what the Bible means by baptism.

Our Christian faith has its roots in Judaism, and to this day Jewish people immerse themselves in something called the Mikveh. This is a ritual bath, often a tank built into a synagogue just as a baptismal tank is built into a church. The Mikveh is used for ritual cleansing of impurity or contamination. The Mikveh is used by women for ritual bathing after menstruation and childbirth, in becoming a Jewish convert, when making a vow to follow God, or as outward demonstration of repenting from a sin. Complete immersion in the "living water" was necessary as a sign of a complete washing away of impurity and contamination.

So when John the Baptist baptized repentant sinners in the River Jordan (John 1:26), perhaps he was saving the people a trip to the Mikveh. Sprinkling people would just not have done the job. It had to be immersion.

Likewise when we are baptized as believers. Complete immersion under the water isn't just following the example of the New Testament, but is identifying with the death and burial (going under the water) and resurrection (coming out of the water) of our Lord Jesus Christ.

> "Therefore we are buried with him by baptism into death, that as Christ was raised up from the dead, by the glory of the Father, even so we also should walk in newness of life."
>
> —Romans 6:4

So What Do You Think?

_____

_____

_____

_____

_____

_____

_____

_____

_____

Without Faith It Is Impossible to Please God

"By faith Abel offered to God a more excellent sacrifice than Cain."
—Hebrews 11:4

"But without faith it is impossible to please Him [God]."
—Hebrews 11:6

In Genesis 4, we find that Adam and Eve's firstborn Cain was a farmer while his young brother Abel raised sheep. Each brought an offering to God. It seems logical that their offerings were in accordance with their occupation. Cain brought an offering of his harvest while Abel sacrificed a firstborn sheep. Abel's offering was accepted by the Lord, but his brother Cain's wasn't.

We often assume Cain's offering was rejected because it wasn't a blood sacrifice like Abel's. But in fact the Bible speaks of many offerings that weren't blood sacrifices, including offerings of the harvest just like Cain's (Exodus 23:19, Deuteronomy 26:1-2). So why was Cain's gift rejected? Could it be that it was not brought in faith like Abel's? That makes sense, doesn't it? It had nothing to do with a blood sacrifice!

So, dear friend, if you want God to accept your tithes and offerings to Him and to receive His blessings on your gifts in return, remember that you must offer them in faith, not out of obligation or just habit.

So What Do You Think?

_____

_____

_____

_____

_____

_____

_____

_____

_____

_____

_____

_____

_____

_____

_____

_____

_____

_____

_____

_____

_____

They Lost Jesus

"When he [Jesus] was 12 they went up to Jerusalem .... as they [Mary and Joseph] returned, the Child Jesus tarried behind ...and Joseph and his mother knew it not...but they supposing him to have been in the company, went one day's journey ...and it came to pass that after 3 days they found Him in the Temple."

—Luke 2:41-46

It took Mary and Joseph one day to miss Jesus but three days to go back and find Him. So it is with us. Our lives are so busy. We focus on the events of the day instead of the presence of the Lord with us. It may be many days before we realize that we are out of fellowship with Him. And it will take us longer than one day to seek the Lord and enjoy His presence again!

This verse teaches me a lot. One day to miss Jesus, but three days to get back into fellowship with Him. So, dear friend, don't let your busy life or distractions lead you away from His presence to begin with and you won't have to spend valuable time seeking to get back to Him.

So What Do You Think?

_____

_____

_____

_____

_____

_____

_____

_____

_____

_____

_____

_____

_____

_____

_____

_____

_____

_____

_____

_____

Rooted, Grounded, and Built

"That Christ may dwell in your hearts by faith; that you being rooted and grounded in love…"

—Ephesians 3:17

"You therefore have received Christ Jesus the Lord, so walk in Him, rooted and built up in Him."

—Colossians 2:6-7

"For we are God's fellow workers; you are God's field, you are God's building."

—1 Corinthians 3:9

"Having been built on the foundation of the apostles and prophets, Jesus Christ Himself being the chief cornerstone, in whom the whole building, being fitted together, grows into a holy temple in the Lord, in whom you also are being built together for a dwelling place of God in the Spirit."

—Ephesians 2:20-22

"You also, as living stones, are being built up a spiritual house…acceptable to God through Jesus Christ."

—1 Peter 2:5

Rooted equals agriculture. Grounded equals construction. When we trust in Jesus Christ as our personal Savior, we are immediately indwelt by the Holy Spirit of God. We are rooted in Christ now and for all eternity.

But to be grounded refers to construction. A building. The apostle Paul in Ephesians 2 tells us that we as the body of Christ are being built into a holy temple and spiritual dwelling place for God Himself. This building is being constructed on the foundation of both the Old and New Testaments (apostles and prophets) with Jesus Christ as the Cornerstone that keeps this construction from collapsing.

So, dear friend, what does this mean? It means that we need to build on our life of faith day by day. And how do we do that? The answer is in the above verses. We must receive Christ the Lord. Walk in Him. Let Christ dwell in our hearts through faith. Let the Holy Spirit rule in us. Only then will we grow into a building acceptable to God through Christ Jesus.

So What Do You Think?

Look to the Clouds

After He [Jesus] said this, He was taken up before their very eyes,
and a cloud hid Him from their sight.

—Acts 1:9 NIV

When we think of clouds, we typically think of impending rain or a storm coming our way. We may not consider clouds as something positive or beautiful unless they are bright white clouds with a very blue sky as a backdrop canvas. Clouds signal an unwelcome interruption of planned out-door activities.

But in the Bible, clouds always symbolize God's divine presence. In fact, God is often described in the Old Testament in terms of being a shade or shelter against the oppressive heat of a burning desert sun (Psalm 91:1; 121:5, Isaiah 4:6; 25:4).

In the book of Acts, we read that Jesus was taken up in a cloud right in front of the disciples. I'm sure they weren't looking at the cloud as something negative. They were looking at Jesus. Another example of God's divine presence as a cloud is when Moses ascended Mount Sinai and the cloud of God's glory covered the mountain (Exodus 24:16). The cloud also led and sheltered the Israelites by day through the wilderness (Exodus14:19), becoming a column of fire at night. The cloud of God's glory is also frequently described as filling the temple, such as at the original dedication of the temple by King Solomon (1 Kings 8:10-11).

Most exciting of all is that we as Christians will one day see the clouds of God's divine presence for ourselves when Jesus comes back just as He left—in a cloud.

Then they will see the Son of Man coming in the clouds with great power and glory.

—Mark 13:26

After that, we who are still alive and are left will be caught up together with them in the clouds to meet the Lord in the air.

— 1 Thessalonians 4:17

So, dear friend, I hope you are ready and eagerly waiting for Jesus to return in the clouds. If so, I will see you there!

So What Do You Think?

_____

_____

_____

_____

_____

_____

_____

_____

_____

_____

_____

_____

_____

_____

Auto Makers Have the Right Idea

But one thing I do, forgetting what Is behind and straining toward
what is ahead, I press on toward the goal.

—Philippians 3:12-14

Designers of automobiles would probably never think of applying this Bible verse to the various models of cars they create. But in fact they do the very thing mentioned in this verse in the design and construction of their vehicles. They always have a very large windshield in the front and a very small rearview mirror.

Interesting! This is exactly what we need to do in our own daily lives. The past is over, and each day is a new beginning in our journey of life. So we need to keep our focus forward toward the road ahead we can see through that large, transparent windshield, not on the tiny view of the road we've already traveled that can be seen in that small rearview mirror.

So, my friend, practice this verse each day as you drive your vehicle by pressing forward with faith, courage, and determination to do what God has designed you to do. Remember there will only ever be one exactly like you on this planet. So accept yourself and be open to the leading of God to guide you into a fruitful life, one of purpose and fulfillment in whatever you do.

So What Do You Think?

_____

_____

_____

_____

_____

_____

_____

_____

_____

_____

_____

_____

_____

_____

_____

_____

_____

_____

_____

God Speaks to Sperm

I praise you, God, for I am fearfully and wonderfully made.

—Psalm 139:14

Oh yes, God does speak to sperm, all 100 million of them, as they are floating around in the dark in a woman's womb. It takes a special sperm to make YOU. God must speak to each sperm: "no, no, no….not you, not you, not you."

But the sperm with the exact components to make YOU, God says "okay…go hit that egg!"

And here you are exactly what God had planned you to be. Any other sperm would have created a different person. God wanted YOU to be exactly like you are so that He can love you, bless you and use you for his Glory. How special we all are.

So my friend, if you think you are not important or your family tells you that "you were a mistake or not planned"…think again. God designed you to be exactly like you are. You are loved.

Enjoy who you are and let God bless you and love you.

So What Do You Think?

_____

_____

_____

_____

_____

_____

_____

_____

_____

_____

_____

_____

_____

_____

_____

_____

_____

_____

_____

_____

_____

_____

Part Three:

Meditations to Help You Smile

More Thoughts to Ponder

Difference Between "Milk" of the Word and "Meat"

Both are protein. But milk has been predigested by someone else. Meat is what you get on your own from the Word of God (Hebrews 5:12-13).

His Glory

In His prayer to the Father at the end of the Last Supper, Jesus says of His disciples, "and the glory which Thou gave Me, I have given them" (John 17:22). Think of it! Jesus Christ has given His glory to every believer in Him. What does that mean? Everything wonderful! Let's live so we are clean vessels through which the Holy Spirit can shine.

Just One Generation Away

We are all only one generation away from idolatry. Just because parents fervently follow the Lord does not guarantee their children will do the same. The prophet Samuel's children did not follow the Lord even though he was a dedicated servant of God (I Samuel 8:3). So, parents, commit your children to the Lord and pray that He will draw them to Himself.

Loveless Marriage?

"My Beloved is mine and I am His" (Song of Solomon 2:16). Get your loving from the Lord through His Word, and you will take the pressure off your significant other to make you happy every minute.

Why Anti-Semitism?

Anti-Semitism is Satan's way of preventing the coming of Messiah and the establishment of His kingdom on this planet. In the Old Testament, Satan was trying to prevent His birth. In the New Testament and over the last two thousand years, it was to prevent not only the rebirth of the State of Israel but the Second Advent of Jesus Christ.

Some Trivia to Help You Smile

Sermon

A good sermon is to have a short beginning and a short ending—
and to have the two as close together as possible.

—George Burns

Santa Claus

Santa has the right idea—visit people only once a year.

—Victor Borge

Health Books

Be careful about reading health books. You may die of a misprint.

—Mark Twain

To Marry

By all means, marry. If you get a good woman or man, you will be
very happy. If you get a bad one, you will become a philosopher.

—Socrates

Shut Up

Until I was thirteen, I thought my name was Shut Up.

—Joe Namath

Life at Fifty

Maybe it's true that life begins at fifty, but everything else starts to
wear out, fall out, or spread out.

—Phyllis Diller

Old Age

I don't feel old. I don't feel anything until noon. Then it's time for my nap.

—Bob Hope

We could certainly slow down the aging process if it had to work its way through Congress.

—Will Rogers

If you think you're over the hill, that's good. The only thing you can do is pick up speed.

—Unknown

Old age are the best years because we've got the kinks out of us, no curfew, and a monthly allowance from Uncle Sam.

—Eleanor Isaacson

Temptation

Don't worry about avoiding temptation. As you grow older, it will avoid you.

—Winston Churchill

Watch Your Step

By the time a man is wise enough to watch his step, he's too old to go anywhere.

—Billy Crystal

Victory

The victory for our Lord Jesus Christ was not only at the cross of Calvary when He died there for the sins of the world. It began in Gethsemane when He said, "Thy will be done."

—Eleanor Isaacson

Crucify

We crucify ourselves between two thieves—the past and the future.

—Unknown

Beauty

Beautiful young people are accidents of nature. Beautiful old people are works of art. It is the result of a good diet, grooming well, a forgiving spirit, and an obedient walk with God.

—Eleanor Isaacson

God Himself

God will always replace what He has taken away, either with something better or with Himself.

—Eleanor Isaacson

Joseph (Genesis 37-50)

Make your dungeon a spiritual sentinel to shape you into a loving, forgiving, and compassionate glorious adult.

—Eleanor Isaacson

Conquering

You can't conquer what you can't confront. So like David, confront your Goliath. Be in charge of your enemies. Confront your abusers, and grow up into your full adulthood.

—Eleanor Isaacson

Being Useful

Never consider whether or not you are of use to God. Remember that when you have trusted in our Lord Jesus Christ as your personal Savior, you are not your own. He has bought you, and you are His to use or not use. So relax in this thought today.

—Eleanor Isaacson

Pessimist

No pessimist ever discovered the secrets of the stars or sailed to unchartered land or opened a new heaven to the human spirit.

—Helen Keller

Post Office

Christians are to be God's post office, delivering the Good News of the gospel of Jesus Christ.

—Eleanor Isaacson

Your Giants

Face the giants in your life. They will all fall down at the Name of Jesus when His name is spoken in faith.

—Eleanor Isaacson

Confess

I John 1:9 says that if we **confess** our sins, He [God] is **faithful** and **just** to **forgive** our sins and **cleanse** us from all unrighteousness. Notice that if we do one thing, God will do four things at the same time.

—Eleanor Isaacson

Your Greatest Fear

Face your greatest fear with God and say, "I'll make it!" When you hit bottom, decide, "It's okay, I'll make it anyway." Look for the good in it all. If you just wait awhile, you will see the good as a result of it all.

—Eleanor Isaacson

Human Love

Human love is just a picture of how beautiful and passionately God loves us. Human love can help us open up to God's love. But human love alone cannot fill the void left by the absence of God's presence.

—Eleanor Isaacson

A Healthy Marriage

A wonderful, healthy, satisfying marriage is made up of a threesome—husband, wife, and God. If God is left out, the marriage will always have something missing. The couple tries to fill that void with a bigger house, better job, more kids, etc. But it never works.

—Eleanor Isaacson

Cemetery

Let's face it! There is a kind of safety in the cemetery where nothing much is happening. We settle into the status quo in our lives. But that is a dead end. What's the answer? Always move ahead, make new goals, start new projects, and continue working and growing into your beautiful destiny.

—Eleanor Isaacson

Hanged Kings

In the book of Judges, we read of six kings being hanged on a tree. The seventh king hanged on a tree was our Lord Jesus Christ when He died for our sins on the cross of Calvary.

—Eleanor Isaacson

Rainbow

If you want a rainbow, you've got to put up with the rain!

—Eleanor Isaacson

Parked Car

You want to move forward? Don't follow a parked car.

—Eleanor Isaacson

Pencil

Life without God is like an unsharpened pencil—no point!

—Eleanor Isaacson

Test

God will always test your faith, but it is always an "open book" test. You can always go to your Bible and find encouragement. And the test isn't over in our lives until we win!

—Eleanor Isaacson

Organ Donor

Be an organ donor. Give your heart to Jesus!

—Eleanor Isaacson

Spiritually Dead

Jesus didn't come to make bad people good, but to make dead (spiritually) people alive. How? When we personally accept His life, death, burial, and resurrection on our behalf, the Bible tells us we've been made alive by faith. We are "born again" in the Spirit of God. We begin a whole new life and attitude.

—Eleanor Isaacson

Opportunity

Opportunity always comes to us wrapped in opposition.

—T.D. Jakes

Stretch our Faith

After God's promises in the Bible have become a reality in our lives, then will follow the tests and problems to stretch our faith and courage.

—Eleanor Isaacson

Hebrews

Men should always make the coffee. He—brews!

—Rabbi Green

Real Faith

Real tested faith will always step out and take risks.

—Eleanor Isaacson

Holiness

To date, nobody has ever drifted into holiness! It takes discipline, vision, and dedication in our daily lives. Holiness is something we won't see in ourselves, but others will notice it.

—David Jeremiah

Failure

Success consists of going from failure to failure without the loss of enthusiasm.

—Winston Churchill

Conviction

One man with conviction will overwhelm a hundred who have only opinions.

—Winston Churchill

Success

The only place where success comes before work is in the dictionary.

—Eleanor Isaacson

Becoming

What you GET by achieving your goals is not as important as what you BECOME by achieving them.

—Zig Ziglar

Hurry

Hurry is not of the devil....it is the devil!

—Carl Jung
1875-1961

The Way to Go

In the middle of the trackless universe, Jesus Christ is the way!

—Selwyn Hughes

Let Me In

Here I am! I stand at the door and knock.

If anyone hears my voice and opens the door, I will come in and eat with him, and he with me.

—Jesus Christ
Revelation 3:20

Something Even Better

Our heavenly Father never takes anything from his children unless he means to give them something better.

—George Muller
1805-1898

Forward

I will go anywhere, provided it is forward.

—David Livingston
1813-1873

Rest

My Presence shall go with you and I will give you rest.

—God
Exodus 33:14

Courage to Do the Right

Let us have faith that right makes might, and in that faith let us to the end, dare to do our duty as we understand it.

—Abraham Lincoln
1809-1865

Security

I am with you always, even to the very end of the age.

—Jesus Christ
Matthew 28:20

About the Author

Born in New Jersey, speaker, author, and WWII survivor Eleanor Isaacson was raised till age thirteen in East Germany. Returning to the USA with neither English nor family, she overcame every obstacle to graduate with a double Bachelor's Degree magna cum laude, become a successful business entrepreneur, and marry renowned scientist Dr. Robert Isaacson. She is also a competitive ballroom dancer with more than 100 first-place wins.

Eleanor has been an inspirational speaker for more than forty years throughout the United States. She was voted "The Speaker of the Year" for the past five years in Lancaster County. She was also awarded an honorary Doctoral Degree from Lancaster Bible College in 2017.

You can contact Eleanor on her website at
www.eleanorisaacson.com.

Read Eleanor's Award-Winning Story!

Dancing from Darkness: A WWII Survivor's Journey to Light, Life, and Redemption
2018 Memoir of the Year by American Writers and
Speakers Association

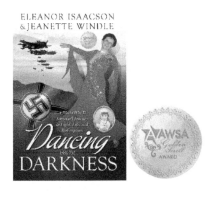

Abandoned as a toddler in Nazi Germany, American-born Eleanor Isaacson survived bombings, starvation, Russian occupation, and a stint as a child smuggler—all before reaching her teens. Escaping just as the Iron Curtain clashed shut, Eleanor soon discovered that "the land of the free" held as much pain and rejection as the life she'd escaped. Deafness and solitude would become the catalyst leading to glorious womanhood, the love of her life, and the beauty of dance. In the process, she would discover that the "invisible Friend" whose presence alone had kept a lost child sane had other names—heavenly Father, loving God, Prince of Peace. A true story too implausible for fiction with every element of a big screen epic—war, danger, starvation, villains, romance, rags-to-riches triumph—along with the most delightful of heroines.

Invite Eleanor to Speak

As a presenter and confident speaker, Eleanor Isaacson is available to speak to various groups, including schools, on a variety of topics including:

- Finding God as a World War II Survivor
- Dealing with Difficult Parents as an Adult
- Vibrant Widowhood
- Positive Attitudes and Nutritional Helps that Can Help You to Be Your Best from the Inside Out.

You can contact Eleanor on her website at
www.eleanorisaacson.com.

Made in the USA
Middletown, DE
26 May 2023

31544400R00099